TEXT BY CATHERINE CLINTON

Life in Civil War America

The coming of the Civil War was not unanticipated because the sectional conflict had been at the center of American politics for several decades before the firing on Ft. Sumter in April 1861. Yet war was a rude awakening for most Americans who had not realized that Lincoln's election in 1860 and secession fever would culminate in armed struggle for Confederate independence. Few imagined that this conflict would escalate into a full-scale bid to destroy slavery and result in waves of African Americans struggling openly for full and equal rights as citizens, many through the dangerous rite of passage as Union soldiers. Hardly anyone imagined that the conflict would result in the kind of total war which would absorb the entire nation for over four years and deprive the country and families of half a million young men, as the wartime generation and those who followed grappled with the several and severe meanings of civil war.

Charlestonians watched the Confederate bombardment of Ft. Sumter from rooftops overlooking the bay. (LC)

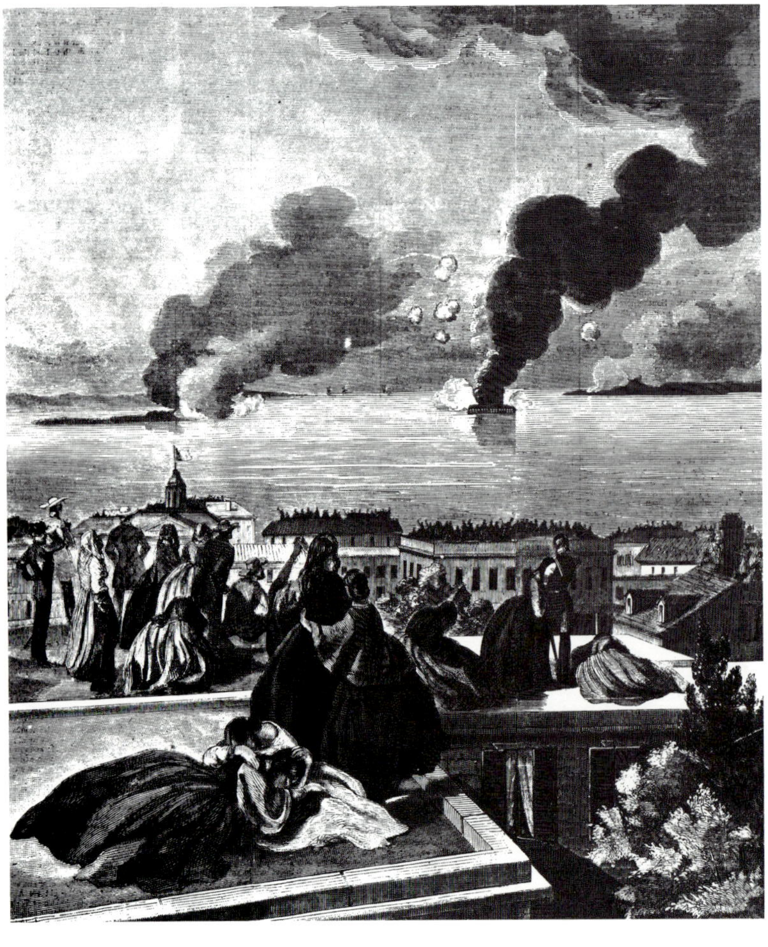

This conflict became all-encompassing, touching the lives of nearly all Americans—slave and free, black and white, native-born and immigrant, property owner and wage earner, man and woman, adult and child—dramatically transformed by this momentous battle to decide the future of the continent. Like many armed engagements, even its name reflected dispute. Lincoln and his government wished to minimize secession, hoping to ignore the sovereignty of the Confederacy. But certainly the "War for the Union," or the "Civil War" was the most popular Yankee appellation. Ardent Confederates had choice names: the "Second American Revolution, "the "War of Northern Aggression," the "War for Southern Independence," the "War for States' Rights." Most Americans, horrified by the way the nation was ripped apart, viewed it as "the Brother's War." Indeed, the conflict deeply divided hundreds of households and thousands of kinship networks when volunteers were needed.

Symbolic of this division was that four of Lincoln's brothers-in-law wore Confederate uniforms. Despite Mary Todd Lincoln's staunch devotion to the Union, her southern relations were loyal to the Confederacy. Other prominent politicians found themselves in complex straits: Senator George B. Crittenden of Kentucky had two sons fighting in the war—one a major general for the Confederacy and the other a major general of the Union. Major Robert Anderson, in charge of federal troops at Ft. Sumter, was the son-in-law of the governor of Georgia. Across the bay he faced his artillery instructor at West Point, Confederate General P. G. T. Beauregard, who fired on his star pupil and former assistant. Many West Point graduates, friends and roommates, faced one another on the battlefield as well as serving alongside military school comrades. (Some wags even believed the outcome of the battle was determined by the class rank of the generals pitted against one another!) Friendship and kinship were rent asunder by the great onslaught of the Civil War.

Childhood was dramatically affected by the onset of war. The overwhelming youth of the armies on both sides and the way young men flocked to battle had a generational impact on America. Out of 2,700,000 federal soldiers, over two million were twenty-one or younger and over a million younger than eighteen. Rough estimates are that 100,000 served in the Union army at fifteen or younger with 300 under thirteen and 25 *under ten.* Most of these extremely youthful volunteers were in the drum and fife corps, but their separation from families and exposure to deprivation and danger could be traumatizing.

In a sampling of a million federal enlistments, only 46,000 soldiers were over twenty-five. Youthful officers became a hallmark of the Union army—with Galusha Pennpacker rising to the rank of brevet major general at seventeen, too

young to vote until the war ended. George Custer rose to this exalted rank at the age of twenty-one and joined six other Union generals in their twenties.

Confederates had equally legendary youths in military service. Brigadier General William P. Roberts of North Carolina rose to his rank at the age of twenty. Boys in gray were equally common, and Confederate troops had disproportionate numbers of teenagers as well, but samplings of rebel ranks indicate that there were larger numbers of men in their twenties and thirties and a larger group of older soldiers, especially as the war wore on. In any case, families were stripped of manpower and communities literally depleted by the war. One town in Wisconsin witnessed 111 of the 250 registered voters volunteering for the army. The farm boys of the midwestern states entered the Union ranks in droves.

But no group was more electrified by the 1860 election than free blacks. Thomas Hamilton, founder of the New

York weekly the *Anglo-African*, had warned in March 1860: "We have no hope from either [of the] political parties. We must rely on ourselves, the righteousness of our cause, and the advance of just sentiments among the great masses of the . . . people." But the majority of African Americans supported Lincoln. The Colored Republican Club of Brooklyn raised a "Lincoln Liberty Tree" in the summer of 1860, and similar signs of African American solidarity dotted the northeastern seaboard and Old Northwest river-

UNION MOBS TARRED AND FEATHERED A PRO-CONFEDERATE NEWSPAPER EDITOR, AS SHOWN IN THIS FRANK LESLIE ILLUSTRATION.

(FW)

sides. Most eligible black voters cast their ballots for Lincoln.

Frederick Douglass crowed over Lincoln's victory: "For fifty years the country has taken the law from the lips of an exacting, haughty and imperious slave oligarchy . . . . Lincoln's election has vitiated their authority, and broken their power." The threat of disunion buoyed black activists during postelection chaos. In the North, they rallied to the cry, "BREAK EVERY YOKE." Blacks saw the split in the Union as a sign that the North could no longer tolerate slaveholders' tyranny.

White Southerners chose to interpret Lincoln's election and the response to secession in equally strong terms. Further, slaveholders feared the undermining of their authority, which armed federal intervention represented. The slave grapevine rattled with the threat of war. In the Deep South, conspiracies and plots spontaneously combusted in the war's first few weeks. On May 14, 1861, a planter in Jefferson County, Mississippi, wrote to the governor concerning his fears: "A plot has been discovered and [alrea]dy three Negroes have gone the way of all flesh or rather paid the penalty by the forfeiture of their lives." He argued that 11,000 slaves surrounding less than a thousand whites might foment devastating insurrection. The plotters' "diabolical" plans included killing white males, capturing white females, and marching "up the river to meet '*Mr. Linkin*' bearing off booty such things as they could carry." Planter paranoia prevailed in the Delta countryside.

By the end of the long hot summer of 1861, a plot was uncovered in Adams

County, where a Mississippi woman reported "that a miserable, sneaking abolitionist has been at the bottom of this whole affair. I hope that he will be caught and burned alive." Alarm ran rampant in the rural interior, where husbands and sons had been lured off to the Confederate army and blacks routinely outnumbered whites twenty to one. Local investigators determined that this home-grown conspiracy was the work of slaves, planning to rise up against masters in the event of federal invasion. By mid-September, Home Guards and Vigilance Committees in Adams County were on the offensive and nearby counties on alert. Reportedly twenty-seven black men were hung. A woman writing from her plantation confided, "It is kept very still, not to be in the papers."

With the outbreak of war, the Confederacy required the utmost cooperation of all her citizens, especially from the sons and daughters of the planter class. The newly formed government did not want hysteria in the countryside and slave owners arming themselves against their own slaves. As a result, evidence of insurrectionary activity was repressed. Despite the protracted efforts of Confederate loyalists to portray only harmony among owner and owned, despite best efforts to rally blacks to the Stars and Bars, we know not all African Americans were devoted servants to Confederate masters, as painted by wartime rhetoric or postwar ideologues.

Equally interesting evidence remains, however, on this question of black loyalty. In New Orleans, Confederate leaders confronted an affluent, articulate, and assimilated free black community. The colored Creoles were in a difficult position when Louisiana left the Union—a people without a country. The mixed-race "mulatto" community emphasized community ties and volunteered to "take arms at a moment's notice and fight shoulder to shoulder with other citizens." A local unit of "colored men" even enrolled in the state militia.

African American men who formed companies and offered themselves for military service, however, were greeted with considerable discomfort by the new southern government, ignored and spurned. The Confederacy dared not allow blacks to serve as soldiers. Free blacks who did volunteer were assigned to projects as teamsters on earthworks projects, building fortifications, and other menial support roles. The loyalties of these free blacks volunteers were considerably divided. Most, like the New Orleans Native Guards, feared that if Confederate independence was achieved without their help, they might be returned to slavery. To safeguard status, they pledged themselves to the Confederate cause— perhaps even aware of the emptiness of such a gesture.

From the very earliest days of the war, slaves were caught in a vicious thrall. Many hoped to escape bondage and fled behind enemy lines. The flooding of Union camps with fugitive slaves was an alarming and unanticipated development for federal officers. Confederates who claimed that slaves were loyal to owners because the system of paternalism fostered mutual dependency were repudiated by a steady stream of black desertions.

Unfortunately, federal soldiers expressed less than sympathetic attitudes toward blacks in bondage, such as the Union man who balked at the suggestion that he was fighting for blacks' freedom and retorted: "I ain't fighting for the damned niggers, I'm fighting for fifteen dollars a month."

Despite such rampant racism among federal troops, African Americans overwhelmingly sided with the Union— indeed, the Native Guards proved their true colors during federal occupation. When Union forces threatened to overrun the Crescent City in the spring of 1862, black troops volunteered to remain behind. They ended up greeting soldiers in blue with jubilation and switching sides effortlessly.

From the earliest days of the war, federal military units employing blacks were organized in South Carolina and Louisiana to capture the runaways and harness their loyalty. Thousands of African Americans were willing to take up arms against the Confederacy. The flood of black volunteers northward from the Confederate states increased dramatically with the Emancipation Proclamation in January 1863. It was a time of tremendous rejoicing for slaves trapped behind Confederate lines. Most thought of New Year's Day with sadness, as it was the time when sales were organized and families separated, nicknamed "Heartbreak Day." But after 1863 the majority of African Americans would celebrate instead of dread this date.

The Union at first resisted the use of blacks as soldiers, although these runaways, who were called "contrabands," were welcomed and employed as teamsters and ditchdiggers to man the engi-

neering and quartermasters' corps. But free blacks persisted and commanders relented, so well over 100,000 black men from Confederate states ran away to join the Union army. By war's end nearly 200,000 African Americans had served under the Union flag.

Despite Confederate efforts to stem the tide, the federals were able to drain plantations of precious manpower and, even more boldly, allow former slaves to return to these plantations as enemy soldiers—an alarming prospect for most planter households. As one former slave soldier reported when he went to see his mistress after the Battle of Nashville, she upbraided him, reminding him of how she nursed him when he was sick, and "'now, you are fighting me!' I said, 'No'm, I ain't fighting you, I'm fighting to get free.'"

Slave women and families, left behind by fathers and husbands, could be thrown into precarious situations when planters discovered "treason" and vented their anger on family members who remained in slavery. One wife left behind in Missouri confided: "They are treating me worse and worse every day. Our child cries for you. Send me some money as soon as you can for me and my child are almost naked." A white commander of a black regiment complained that planters forbade wives and children to see these black men in blue and prevented all communication, especially the flow of wages back to the plantation home. Some African American soldiers, driven to desperation by such treatment, risked all to return and retrieve families, such as Spottswood Rice, who plotted from his hospital bed to rescue his children: "Be assured that I will have you if it cost me my life." One Kentucky woman spirited her several children away, only to be halted on the road by her master's son-in-law, "who told me that if I did not go back with him he would shoot me. He drew a pistol on me as he made this threat. I could offer no resistance as he constantly kept the pistol pointed at me." Forcing her to return to slavery at gunpoint, the man kept her seven-year-old as hostage to ensure that she wouldn't run away again.

Black women of the South, like white women, suffered when menfolk went off to war. Jane Welcome wrote a letter complaining to Lincoln: "I wont to know sir if you please wether I can have my son relest from the arme he is all the subport I have now his father is Dead and his brother was all the help that I had." The president's office replied: "The interests of the service will not permit that your request be granted." But evidence also suggests that many black women willingly bade slave men off to war. Although fearing for soldiers' safety and dreading repercussions, they saw this occasion as a golden opportunity to secure future freedom. Only 11 percent of the black population within the country was free, and the majority of slaves knew military service was a means of liberation. The masses of African Americans who joined the Union both undermined the Confederate cause and strengthened the fight for emancipation. Blacks in the Union armed forces struck a vital blow to

white southern pride, all the while crippling the plantation economy. In the North, persistence on the part of the free black community prodded the federal government into accepting black military potential.

When the war broke out in 1861, the North placed its faith in moral superiority and material advantage. The Union was a powerful image, and Lincoln used his "house" metaphor, hoping to keep the national family together. The Union wanted to impress upon its sibling rival that it possessed more improved farmland than the South and more soldiers in its growing population than did the Confederacy. Southern superiority in exports, almost exclusively cotton, could be abolished with the blockade. The North had over 125,000 industrial firms and the South had less than 20,000. New York State alone manufactured four times the value of manufactured products as did the entire Confederacy. One *county* in Connecticut manufactured more firearms than all the southern states combined.

The North had more and better ports, superior canals, and generally better transportation. Although the United States boasted one of the largest railroad networks in the world, less than one third of its tracks were in the southern states—and 96 percent of American trains were manufactured in the North. Southern shipbuilding was considerably inferior to the size and scope of northern naval capabilities. Financial centers, especially sophisticated trade in bonds, were concentrated along the northeastern seaboard. Southern farmers were less commercially acclimated than the New England, Middle Atlantic, and Old Northwest homesteaders, with closer

ties to eastern markets, fed by flatboat and steamer trade.

At the same time, most white southern volunteers had been trained in local militias and were better equipped to forage from their hunting expertise. Further, the Confederacy declared its independence, which meant it could conduct a defensive war against Yankee invaders, a far simpler tactic than the conquest required for Union victory. The numbers were reputedly against Confederate victory, but the spirit was strong, and the North had not anticipated just how entrenched and determined Confederate rebels had become.

THE NORTHERN
HOME FRONT

The northern home front rallied to the Union cause with remarkable fervor considering that Lincoln was elected by a minority and many blamed this first Republican president for the outbreak of war. When South Carolina seceded, much like the fireworks over states' rights during Andrew Jackson's presidency, when John C. Calhoun resigned as vice-president, many Americans thought it would be another family squabble rather than the full-scale conflict that ensued. If the battle was a brothers' war, then Northerners cast themselves as the good and dutiful sons loyally serving the interests of the Founding Fathers, unlike their rebel siblings, who were willing to turn their backs on ancestors, to grasp avari-

PATRIOTIC PENNSYLVANIA LASSES POSING WHILE SEWING A FLAG AT THE PHILADELPHIA ACADEMY OF FINE ARTS IN 1861.

(LLOYD OSTENDORF COLLECTION)

ciously for themselves alone. One colonel explicitly expressed this family metaphor to his troops: "This great nation is your father, and has greater claim on you than anybody else in the world . . . . This great father of yours is fighting for his life, and the question is whether you are going to stay and help the old man out, or whether you're going to sneak home and sit down by the chimney corner in ease and comfort while your comrades by the thousands and hundreds of thousands are marching, struggling, fighting and crying on battlefields and in prison pens to put down this wicked rebellion and save the old Union." And so paternal fealty—devotion to the fatherland—pushed many a northern soldier onward and kept many hitched to army life despite hardship.

Because so many believed in the Union cause, they met the call for sacrifice as thousands took up arms. Panic spread fear in the streets of Washington, D.C., during the spring of 1861. Lincoln responded with a show of force, increasing his authority to meet the crisis. Following Lincoln's suspension of the writ of habeus corpus, nearly 13,000 arrests were made between 1861 and 1863 to maintain order. All individual interests and liberties were suborned to the interests of the state—the preservation of the Union. Women, most of all, needed to pledge their faith to the Union—and only through such steadfast feminine support could victory emerge.

Yankee females expressed their sentiments openly in letters to one another. Ellen Wright of Massachusetts wrote to her friend Lucy McKim in Pennsylvania: "Away with melancholy is the tune for us nowadays—Chirp up . . . stir the fire—relish your lemonade and 'make believe' a little longer." Many of these girls found it harder and harder to make believe as the death toll rose. Ellen Wright commiserated when Dick and William (Bev) Chase, her cousins, decided to enlist in 1862. She wanted her friend Lucy to join her so they could become nurses. When Dick died at Murfreesboro, she bitterly confessed,

"There is nothing earthly worth a life of a young man like Dick." Wright was perhaps even more shattered when Bev, too, became a casualty of war. Many Yankee women strongly supported the war without bloodthirsty declarations or fiery calls for enlistment.

The patriotism of northern women was frequently contrasted to the fierce chauvinism of female Confederates, as one Yankee primly defended: "The feelings of Northern women are rather deep than violent; their sense of duty is quiet and constant rather than headlong or impetuous impulse." This notion of female devotion was integral to the Union image of itself. Volunteerism as the secular faith swept men into the army and women into war work, including the nursing corps.

Women as caretakers of the family well prepared them for nursing in theory. In reality, it was considered improper for women to have such intimate contact with strangers. Hospitals, far from the bastions of cleanliness and order we hope they are today, had no such illusions in the nineteenth century. These institutions were filled with filth and carnage during the antebellum period, and wartime dramatically escalated the degree of exposure to unpleasantries. Christian-sponsored as well as secular efforts eased women's entrance into controversial new roles, but it was still an uphill battle for women to contribute outside their own homes and family.

The two largest voluntary organizations in the North during this period were the Christian Commission and the Sanitary Commission. The Christian Commission wanted to "promote the spiritual good of the soldiers in the army and incidentally, their intellectual improvement and social

(© INDIANAPOLIS MUSEUM OF ART, JAMES E. ROBERTS FUND)

and physical comfort." Leaders of the Young Men's Christian Association, temperance advocates, and members of Sunday school unions channeled their zeal into this national organization. Spiritual welfare was the primary focus of the group, a unified effort that crossed sectarian lines. The board was filled with politicians and philanthropists and held its annual meetings in the House of Representatives, attended by important dignitaries, including, on at least one occasion, Lincoln himself.

The Christian Commission provided a much needed coordinating system, which funneled supplies to soldiers. By 1864 over 2,000 "delegates" were involved in the campaign, distributing more than half a million Bibles, half a million hymnals, and over four million "knapsack

THE U.S. CHRISTIAN COMMISSION ESTABLISHED DOZENS OF BRANCHES TO DISTRIBUTE SUPPLIES TO NEEDY SOLDIERS.

(LC)

and passing out religious tracts. They believed in the personal touch, a hands-on promotion of Christian values. (The social gospel philosophy at the end of the century grew directly out of this movement.) Their heartfelt mission was to touch the lives of Union soldiers, to replace the families from which they had been taken. Jane Swisshelm, who volunteered to work in Union hospitals, described an experience:

"'What is your name?' a wounded solider at Fredericksburg asked.

'My name is mother,' she replied. 'Mother. Oh my God! I have not seen my mother for two years. Let me feel your hand.'"

Swisshelm reported that some men feared their emotive responses might be misconstrued as immature behavior, but she comforted most with the thought that their soldiering was a test of their manhood, and after being wounded, they deserved maternal care.

The Sanitary Commission was a formidable institution which perhaps drew strength from its diversity. Hundreds of ladies' aid societies solicited and donated

books." Funds were solicited directly, and Yankee cities were consistently generous, especially in the wake of a major battle. During the Wilderness Campaign, Pittsburgh contributed $35,000, Philadelphia $50,000, and Boston $60,000. Over the course of the war, the commission collected nearly $6 million. Delegates were not only generous solicitors but supportive dispensers of goods and care: handing out fresh fruits and sweets, taking dictation from men too ill to write home, holding prayer meetings,

CIVILIANS ENTHUSIASTICALLY SUPPORTED EFFORTS TO CHEER AND COMFORT UNION SOLDIERS— "OUR BOYS AWAY FROM HOME"—AS SHOWN IN THIS 1861 LITHOGRAPH.

(COLLECTION OF THE NEW YORK HISTORICAL SOCIETY)

hospital supplies. Scores of dedicated women workers saw their missions transformed from genteel taskmistresses to women warriors. Many took to the podium as well, like Mary Livermore, a teacher turned writer whose stumping on behalf of the commission reaped tremendous rewards. Feeding the soldiers became a challenge, and a manual on diet and cooking prepared by Annie Wittenmyer became a standard and much appreciated contribution. Wittenmyer did on-the-job training as superintendent of all army kitchens. Mary Shelton, Jane Hoge, and Eliza Porter were equally significant contributors to the commission's success.

The Sanitary Commission also established a transport service to evacuate sick and wounded to hospitals. Eliza Howland and her sister Georgeanne Woolsey contributed, along with their five other sisters and mother, to nursing soldiers. Katherine Prescott Wormeley gave up her role as mere philanthropist to jump into the fray of service, working in one of the commission's "floating hospitals." Wormeley wrote of her female comrades, "They are as efficient, wise, active as cats, merry, light-hearted, thoroughbred and without the fearful tone of self-devotion which sad experience makes one expect in benevolent women." One of the most dynamic women working within and outside the Sanitary Commission's domain, Mary Anne Bickerdyke was so beloved by Union soldiers that they nicknamed her "mother." During her four years, she wore a Quaker

bonnet as she crisscrossed the border states, cleaning up the messes the army left behind. Eventually, Bickerdyke became so concerned with the fatality rate in hospitals that she set up facilities all too near the battlefield, which made many commanders nervous. Bickerdyke was a colorful figure and widely admired. Dorothea Dix was an equally spirited and headstrong leader of a group of nurses, as many of these ventures were privately funded. But estimates are as high as two thousand women serving as nurses to the

Union army. After a brief stint of service in Washington, Louisa May Alcott returned home to Massachusetts and penned her *Hospital Sketches*, followed by *Little Women* and other popular titles.

Clara Barton began her work with Massachusetts troops and soon traveled far and wide to serve at the front. She showed up at Antietam in an oxcart loaded down with supplies. She tried to maintain her ladylike composure but complained that the conditions were nei-

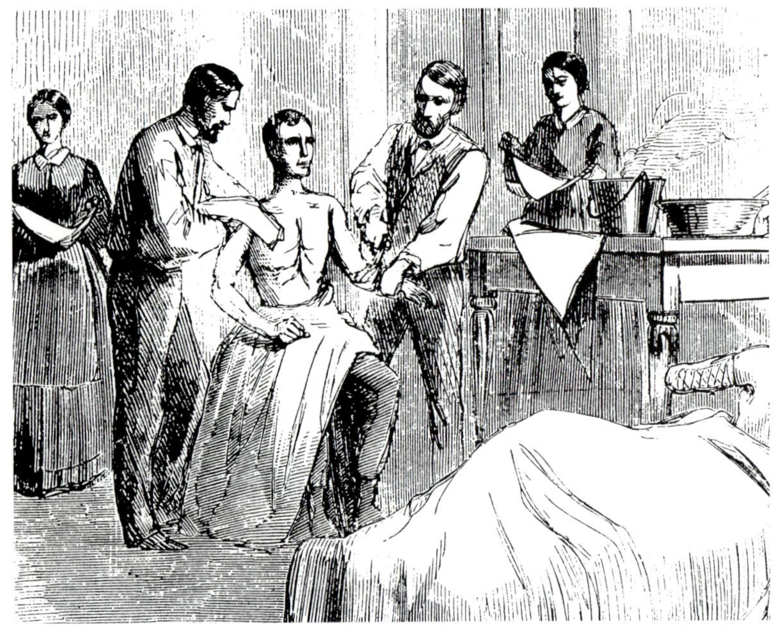

Although soldiers welcomed the nurses, individual Union men raised objections, especially about their own wives and relations endangering themselves in army hospitals. Ulysses S. Grant said he would send his wife home if she did not stay out of the camp hospital. Nevertheless, tributes rather than threats were more common. Frederick Law Olmsted praised the "glorious women" in the Sanitary Commission, commenting, "God knows what we should have done without them, they have worked like heroes night and day." Women worked against the prejudices of men and earned high praise.

ther fit for men nor women on the front lines, recounting a story of a wounded soldier shot in her arms as she gave him water. Barton suffered two severe bouts of illness during the war, and estimates are as high as one in ten female nurses succumbed to fatigue or disease and was forced into bed rest. Several suffered permanent impairment, and a few died of complications following prolonged nursing service.

In 1863 Sanitary Commission worker Mary H. Thompson opened the Chicago Hospital for Women and Children to provide an alternative for female nurses and doctors. Later that year the New York Medical College for Women took in its first class, and the struggle for medical education accelerated with wartime challenges. Men's biases did not fall by the wayside but were suspended because of

13

Union Nurses Prevail
Confronting the Horrors of War

*S*ophronia Bucklin was like many young women of her generation—bright, committed, patriotic. When the Civil War broke out, this schoolteacher from Auburn, New York, applied to be a nurse in the Union army. Dorothea Dix had been appointed superintendent of women nurses in June 1861 and exacted strict requirements from those under her supervision. Only women over thirty and "plain in appearance" needed to apply. Despite Bucklin's youth, she must have passed muster with Dix, as she was accepted into the nursing corps and began her service at the Judiciary Square Hospital in Washington.

Bucklin found her initial encounter with male medical staff challenging. Female nurses discovered that most military officers and surgeons were resentful of women's presence in Union hospitals. Bucklin served the needs of her patients with a stiff upper lip but confided that she felt the army doctors were "determined by a systematic course of ill treatment . . . to drive women from the service."

Nevertheless, Bucklin, like thousands of women volunteers, triumphed in the battles against the male bureaucracy and made invaluable contributions. Her vivid memoir, *In Hospital and Camp: A Woman's Record of Thrilling*

Incidents Among the Wounded in the Late War (1869), provides gripping detail. Bucklin's graphic descriptions of the horrors of war encountered by this genteel generation of ladies are compelling:

About the amputating tent lay large piles of human flesh—legs, arms, feet and hands. They were strewn promiscuously about—often a single one lying under our very feet, white and bloody—the stiffened members seeming to be clutching offtimes at our clothing. . . . Death met us on every hand. It was a time of intense excitement. Scenes of fresh horror rose up before us each day. Tales of suffering were told, which elsewhere would have

well-nigh frozen the blood with horror. We grew callous to the sight of blood. . . . A soldier came to me one day, when I was on the field, requesting me to dress his wound, which was in his side. He had been struck by a piece of shell, and the cavity was deep and wide enough to insert a pint bowl. . . . Often they [the patients] would long for a drink of clear, cold water, and lie on the hard ground, straining the filthy river water through closely set teeth. So tortured were we all, in fact, by this thirst, which could not be allayed that even now, when I lift to my lips a drink of pure cold water, I cannot swallow it without thanking God for the priceless gift.

wartime necessity. Certainly the hard work women provided—to nurse and comfort, to feed and forage, to clothe and cleanse—left men free to carry on crushing burdens of war.

The northern economy, profoundly affected if not transformed by war, thrived. The United States offered extraordinary opportunity, and the North

remained a beacon for liberty. One in five of the twenty million northerners was foreign-born. Even more amazing, almost a quarter million per year continued to emigrate to the United States, almost all to the North.

Land remained the greatest lure. Over 70 percent of the northern population resided on farms and over half of

northern wage earners worked the land. The family farm was the dream not just of immigrants, but of a majority of Americans. Many thousands of immigrants bypassed eastern urban centers to come to the midwestern farmlands, trying to earn enough at day labor to buy their own land. Wartime legislators pushed to fulfill this dream. In 1862 Congress passed the Homestead Act, which allowed individuals to settle on 160 acres of land. After laying claim and working their claim for five years, homesteaders obtained deeds. In this way 2.5 million acres were distributed. Over 15,000 new farms sprang up in Minnesota, Wisconsin, Iowa, Kansas, and Nebraska during wartime.

Most of the immigrants landing in America did not settle on farms, and very few made any transition to land ownership without several years as wage laborers. Immigrants entering the United States were usually deposited in urban centers and ports, overcrowded and overpriced for recently arrived greenhorns. Surprisingly, the war provided some means of upward mobility. Immigrants could earn $13 a month by joining the Union army. By 1862, nearly 80,000 New Yorkers out of a population of 816,000 had joined up. Rural regions as much as urban centers responded to the call to arms: Illinois contributed 197,000 volunteers, Iowa 70,000, and over 75,000 enlisted from Wisconsin. Itinerant farm workers were the first to go, as an Iowa farmer explained: "Our hired man left to enlist just as corn planting commenced, so I shouldered my hoe and have worked ever since. I guess my services are just as acceptable as his."

Ironically, farm production was not hard hit but accelerated tremendously during the war. Reaper sales grew 300 percent in response to increased demand.

Consequently, farmers increased their output and, in addition, plentiful harvests contributed to the doubled export of foodstuffs to Europe. The war stimulated new stock and production. With the cotton blockade, northern farmers turned to alternatives, and the wool trade exploded: the number of sheep in northern states grew from 15 million in 1860 to over 32 million in 1866.

Armies in the field were not just in the market for food and clothing. Animals were a major resource for the war effort. Prices for horses pushed slowly upward, from $100 at the outset to $185 by war's end. The Union army used up approximately 500 horses per day by war's end so that despite efforts to supply the insatiable demand, the horse population in the Union dropped by nearly half a million. Mules were as much in demand as horses. The production of cattle and hogs boomed, but demand outstripped supply throughout the war years in the North. Increased consumption seemed not limited just to the army; a general upward trend in meat eating marked the war years. The hog population in the North declined by nearly 3 million during the war years and the production of cows slowed by nearly 800,000 in the last year of the war. The meatpacking industry naturally boomed, and the transportation industry exploded. Wartime witnessed the expansion of the railroad, including suc-cessful completion of the transcontinental railroad in 1864.

Businessmen and entrepreneurs, thrown into confusion by the outbreak of war, finally hit their stride by 1862. Although over 3,000 companies failed in the first twelve months of the war and an income tax was introduced in 1861, the economy began to bounce back as manu-facturing thrived. For example, in Philadelphia, the growth of factories marked rapid expansion: fifty-eight new factories in 1862, fifty-seven in 1863, and sixty-three in 1864. The shoe and textile industry grew, and the war ushered in standardized sizes for clothing. The num-ber of sewing machines in use doubled between 1861 and 1865.

The same year that the war erupted a successful young Scot named Andrew Carnegie formed the Columbia Oil Company. After drilling on the Allegheny yielded 20 barrels a day in 1857, the petroleum industry was poised to launch itself. The young John D. Rockefeller had built himself an oil refinery on the Cuyahoga River in Cleveland, Ohio. (Both Carnegie and Rockefeller bought

THE GENERAL STORE BECAME A CENTER FOR WAR NEWS AS WELL AS A PLACE TO BARTER AND BUY SUPPLIES.

(USAMHI)

themselves substitutes rather than get drafted.) The Comstock Lode near Virginia City, Nevada, provided its owners with $15 million worth of ore annually.

But as business grew, so did speculation and graft. Smuggling became a particularly lucrative part of the northern economy as colonels and quartermasters engineered illicit deals with planters in the southern states. When cotton was ten to twenty cents a pound in Memphis in 1864, it sold for over $1 a pound in Boston. Conversely, while salt sold for $1.25 in the North, an identical amount cost $60 in the southern states.

Certainly inflation hit in the North, and wages were unable to keep pace. While a dozen eggs cost fifteen cents in 1861, by 1864 the price had risen to twenty-five cents. The average daily wage (pegged to a male worker) rose from $1 to only $1.25. While business boomed, labor did not fare so well. Clothing manufacturing thrived, but

MACHINERY AND PATRIOTISM FUELED THE BOOM IN CLOTHING MANUFACTURE.

(HARPER'S WEEKLY)

seamstresses certainly did not. The six-day-a-week, fourteen-hour day netted a seamstress a week's wages of under $2. Northern workers found a 20 percent decline in real earnings as a result of wartime inflation. The wartime labor surplus did not shift into labor shortage until 1862. By the later years of the war, many women replaced men in the fields throughout the North. One observer watched "a stout matron whose sons are in the army with her team cutting hay. . . . She cut seven acres with ease in a day, riding leisurely on her cutter." This ease and leisure was not typical. The majority of Yankee women, like poor seamstresses, struggled for economic survival during hard times. Females increased their proportion of the manufacturing work force (from one-fourth to one-third) but were confined to low-paying sectors, and because of inequities in pay, their increase depressed manufacturing wages. During the last year of the war, real wages in many trades returned to prewar levels and the North was plagued with the problem of worker unrest resulting in violence, strikes, and other labor disputes. Most of these slowdowns and strikes were met with armed resistance and government intervention.

When workers at a munitions factory in Cold Spring, New York, went on strike, the factory owner was able to call in the army to throw strike leaders into jail and restore order. Dock workers in New York were stripped of their pay and locked in the yards when they tried to use organizing tactics. Army troops were brought in and arsenal workers labored at bayonet point in Nashville, Tennessee, after threatening a walkout. "Free labor" had been a battle cry of the Republican party, but once the war was under way labor found itself in the government's thrall and less free than at any other time in the history of labor organization. Railroad engineers, munitions workers, and stevedores were especially vulnerable, as the Union government tolerated no dissent in these war-related industries.

Unrest on the civilian front became an increasing problem as the war wore on. In the wake of northern defeat at Bull Run, over 90,000 men enlisted in less than a month, and over half a million volunteered by November. But when calls for troops were renewed in the summer of 1862, 300,000 recruits were desperately needed. Each recruit received a $100 bounty from the federal government. As each community and state set its own quotas and paid its own bounties, recruits might be paid as much as $500 to enlist. But even these financial incentives were increasingly unsuccessful.

Bounty jumping and hiring substitutes increased with the publication of the death lists. More and more men sought alternatives to joining up. Draft resistance became widespread, and Canada welcomed almost 100,000 men during wartime; almost a third were deserters. Draft dodgers who escaped used the "skedaddle quickstep" as it was called, which reached such epidemic proportions that states such as Iowa passed laws against young men emigrating without passes and the federal government forced Canada to restrict immigration. Nearly 800,000 were called in four drafts between the summer of 1863 and spring of 1865. During this same period 200,000 failed to report and an equal number of deserters left the ranks.

By as early as August 1862 it was impossible to fulfill state quotas. Accommodating doctors were willing to sell certificates of unfitness. In response, the press aggressively published "cowards lists" to shame men into uniform. At the same time civilian agitation was a dangerous proposition for recruiters. When Congress passed the Conscription Act in March 1863, all men between twenty and forty-five were required to register.

Feelings against the draft were exacerbated by the provision that allowed men who could afford it to pay $300 and buy their way out of army service. By the summer of 1863, over 26,000 substitutions had been purchased. Widespread dissent festered, erupting into violence in New York City in July 1863.

When names of draftees were drawn on July 11, on the heels of victories at Gettysburg and Vicksburg, where the Union had sustained devastating losses, protesters were unwilling to make further sacrifices. Democratic agitators stirred protesters into a frenzy with radical rhetoric. New York governor Horatio Seymour proclaimed "that the bloody and treasonable and revolutionary doctrine of public necessity can be proclaimed by a mob as well as by a government." Mobs of unskilled workers, many Irish laborers and their families, roamed the city to exact a toll beginning July 12, and vigilantism and violence followed in their wake.

The violence was extreme and politically motivated—draft offices and merchants were favorite targets. Vandals

broke into Brooks Brothers and helped themselves to expensive clothing, contemptuous of the moneyed classes. Draft offices were burned, recruiters were targeted, and any well-dressed bystander might be seized and attacked as a "$300 man." Store windows were smashed and looted and recruiters' homes were burned. For three days the rampage continued, nearly unabated.

A special brutality and vengeance was reserved for blacks during this violent spree. Racism reared its ugly head and devoured all sense and reason during these riots. Black homes, boardinghouses, churches, and even a black orphanage were burned to the ground. Lynchings were perpetrated while the police remained helpless. The chief of police was beaten unconscious as his men and federal soldiers attempted to restore order. Diarist George Templeton Strong described the mayhem on July 14: "Fire bells clanking as they have at intervals through the evening . . . . Shops were cleaned out and a black man hanged in Carmine Street for no offense but that of *negritude*." On the fourth day of the riot, troops marched in from Gettysburg to help put down the violence. Over 100 people were killed, hundreds more injured, and it took over forty regiments ringing the city to restore order.

Following the draft riots, African Americans fled New York City in large numbers, which reduced the labor pool and improved white wages. The city council voted $2 million to buy substitutes for any policeman, fireman, or member of the militia who was drafted and couldn't afford to pay. Additionally, any New Yorker who could prove that enlistment would impoverish his family was granted a substitute stipend to fight off the draft. Records indicate that few of those caught committing crimes and mayhem during the riot had criminal records and nearly a third of the male participants were not themselves threatened by the draft but merely sympathetic to the protest. Women and children, and especially immigrants, played a disproportionate role in the vio-

lent uprising. Most grand juries refused to indict those arrested, and few received any punishment for their violent acts and even the murders that resulted.

New York City was not alone in its violent uprising. Disturbances broke out in Boston and Troy of a similar character, but none were as bloody and destructive as this draft riot for three long days in July. Massive protests in Chicago's roughest ward, "The Patch" turned out nearly three thousand to protest the draft. When arrests were made, bricks and bottles rained down on the police, who released their captives. When a provost marshal decided to bring in soldiers to quell the riots, workers from a local quarry met the men with clubs and stones. Throughout

Disorder and unrest plagued the Union in a variety of spheres during wartime. Most vexing were the border states, which fostered guerrilla warfare at its most vicious. Missouri was contested terrain throughout the war, with two governments—Confederate and federal—wrestling for control of the population. This state suffered the second largest number of armed encounters (after Virginia) and was a land awash with blood from decades of violence. Union guerrilla leader James H. Lane began by targeting homes that hosted rebel forces but ended with the wholesale plunder of towns and counties. His even more bloody opponent, Confederate Captain William C. Quantrill, began his career opposing slavery but ended as a leader of the Bushwhackers, Confederate guerrillas. He launched a raid on Lawrence, Kansas, an antislavery stronghold, on August 21, 1863, marching nearly five hundred of his men into the town in the early morning hours. Reputedly, while Quantrill breakfasted, his men butchered nearly 150 men and boys, most unarmed, while women and children were forced to witness the barbaric executions. The town was burned to the ground except the saloon, which they looted and left standing.

the North local politicians faced increasingly impossible dilemmas—to keep their constituents happy while meeting war demands from the federal government. Union troops were called into the mining districts of Pennsylvania because Irish miners felt as abused by the draft recruiters as they had by English landlords. When quotas weren't met and disorder threatened, Lincoln cautioned the Pennsylvania governor that saving face was important but not at further political costs—and the unfilled slots were stuffed with men who had once lived or even been born in those mining counties where eligible immigrants resisted recruiters.

CONSCIENTIOUS OBJECTORS AND THE UNION

Many groups that had fought long and hard to defeat slavery, most notably the Society of Friends (known as Quakers), were thrown into a crisis with the outbreak of war. Although most wanted the slave power defeated and the Confederacy restored to the Union, many Quakers were devout pacifists. Quaker abolitionists had spearheaded campaigns protesting the Mexican War in 1848. Lincoln's call to arms in 1861, even for a good cause, created a dilemma for devout Quakers.

The Union created many loopholes for those drafted. The payment of $300 could delay conscription—but only by securing a substitute, a practice frowned upon by members of the Society of Friends, could military service be permanently avoided.

Moral objections were dismissed by recruiters, as men were forced into the army despite religious convictions. Cyrus Pringle, a Quaker from Burlington, Vermont, described his experience in July 1863, compelled to enlist against his will. The Union army was desperate for able-bodied men and wouldn't allow Quaker draftees the luxury of a conscience, as Pringle complained in his diary about debates with officers: "They are utterly unable to comprehend the pure Christianity and spirituality of our principles. They have long stiffened their necks in their own strength. They have stopped their ears to the voice of the Spirit, and hardened their hearts to his influences. They see no duty higher than that to country. What shall we receive at their hands?" Pringle and his fellow Quakers were held in the guardhouse, pending an appeal to Washington. The response from headquarters was disappointing to the pacifists: "The President, though sympathizing with those in our situation, felt bound by the Conscription Act, and felt liberty, in view of his oath to execute laws, to do no more than detail us from active service to hospital duty, or to the charge of the colored refugees."

An even better organized and adamant opposition to war service was begun by the Shakers, followers of Mother Ann Lee. Nearly 6,000 Shakers lived in twenty settlements scattered throughout the North. Church elders sent their representatives directly to Washington to plead their cause: "As we have received the grace of God in Christ, by the gospel, and are called to follow peace with all men, we cannot, consistent with our faith and conscience, bear the arms of war for the purposes of shedding the blood of any,

ELDER FREDERICK W. EVANS

(COURTESY OF HANCOCK SHAKER VILLAGE, PITTSFIELD, MA)

or do anything to justify or encourage it in others." They demanded total financial exemption, which Secretary of War Edwin M. Stanton refused. But when Shaker elder Frederick Evans pointed out that pension payments to veterans of the War of 1812 were owed to scores of men within his community who had become Shakers following military service and that these payments would create an enormous financial penalty, Stanton relented. If the Shakers were granted total immunity, the sum would be forgiven, a bargain federal authorities happily approved. Shakers were the only group granted such a sweeping exemption.

Disorder and unrest plagued the Union in a variety of spheres during wartime. Most vexing were the border states, which fostered guerrilla warfare at its most vicious.

This senseless slaughter of civilians led Union General Thomas Ewing to issue Order No. 11, which required the evacuation of four Missouri counties while Union guerrillas, known as Jayhawkers, had their revenge. A sympathetic federal officer condemned the exodus: "It is heart sickening to see what I have seen here." He went on to decry the looting and pillaging, while near naked families stumbled onto the barren prairie. Confederates retaliated with renewed efforts to stage a coup against Union authorities, and Confederate General Sterling Price invaded with 12,000 troops. Rebel forces were turned back at the Battle of Pilot's Knob before being chased all the way from northeastern Missouri back into Arkansas. Many stragglers followed Quantrill to Texas, but the spirit of counterrebellion had been broken. Missouri guerrillas splintered into bands, none more infa-

talize on its victories and press for peace. Confederate raider Jubal Early roamed the northern countryside and on July 30 demanded a ransom of half a million dollars to spare the town of Chambersburg, Pennsylvania. When the townspeople failed to pay, Early torched the business district and destroyed the heart of the city. That very same day, Union General Ambrose E. Burnside's scheme to tunnel under Confederate lines and blow his enemies up with gunpowder backfired. The tunnel exploded and over a thousand troops surrendered after being caught in a terrible "crater." The federals lost nearly 5,000 troops in the fiasco. Horace Greeley complained, "Our bleeding, bankrupt and almost dying country longs for peace, shudders at the prospect of further wholesale devastation, of new rivers of human blood." Indeed, as the war dragged into its fourth year, Lincoln looked to the South, to General William T. Sherman to crush the southern spirit, which was bending but refused to break. The surprise of Lincoln's reelection in November 1864 invigorated Union efforts to defeat the Confederate bid for independence once and for all.

mous than "Bloody Bill" Anderson, who was said to ride into battle with a necklace of Union scalps round his neck, encouraging his men to mutilate the bodies of victims. Although a populist uprising against the Union never materialized in Missouri, guerrilla fighters, such as Frank and Jesse James, fought on for the Confederate cause, fomenting rebellion in the interior, creating panic among civilians caught in the crossfire of war on the northern frontier.

By 1864, the North grimly faced another year of battle, and Lincoln's chances looked slim. Confederates took advantage of the Union's inability to capi-

AN 1864 ANTI-LINCOLN POSTER FOR THE PRESIDENTIAL CAMPAIGN.

(THE LINCOLN MUSEUM, FT. WAYNE, INDIANA)

THE SOUTHERN HOME FRONT

The willingness of the planter class to donate all, including loved ones and family members, to the Confederate cause

Citizens gather at the Hanover Junction railroad station and wait for news of the battle.

(LC)

has become a part of Civil War folklore. Indeed, there are many examples of aristocratic parents—those who could well have afforded to pay for substitutes—coaxing sons to war. Evidence abounds that southern patriotism and a sense of honor spurred the wealthy elite into action. Equally poignant, many families were devastated by the painful divides the war provoked. Septima M. Collis reported in her memoir: "I never fully realized the fratricidal character of the conflict until I lost my idolized brother Dave of the Southern army one day, and was nursing my Northern husband back to life the next."

Despite the threat of divided loyalty, Confederate nationalism prevailed and rabid chauvinism flourished among the landed gentry. One Selma belle broke her engagement because her fiancé did not enlist before their proposed wedding day. Support for the rebellion created a strange mix of symbols and images for southern whites. Confederate manhood demanded prolonged separation from the glorified household and, ironically, absence from those very loved ones men pledged to protect. But by individual forfeit, all households might be protected, so private

Recruiting in the Shenandoah Valley for enlistment in the Confederate army.

(FW)

Equipment by W. L. Sheppard. Depiction of the elaborate preparations made for departure into the Confederate army.

(MC)

gain was sacrificed to the collective good.

The South nurtured extremity and zeal, encouraging the press to promote stories of female vigilance. The *Raleigh Register* reported an incident in September 1863: "A young lady was engaged to be married to a soldier in the army. The soldier suddenly returned home. 'Why have you left the army?' she inquired of him. 'I have found a substitute,' he replied. 'Well, sir, I can follow your example, and find a substitute, too. Good Morning.' And she left him in the middle of the room, a disgraced soldier." Women might be sentimental, but they could not let fears and personal concerns interfere with the Confederate cause. The weight of victory rested heavily on the plantation matrons' shoulders.

Virginian Margaret Junkin Preston described her husband's letters home: "Such pictures of horrors as Mr. P. gives! Unnumbered dead Federal soldiers cover the battle field, one hundred in one gully, uncovered and rotting in the sun, they were all strewn along the roadside. And dead horses everywhere by the hundred. Hospitals crowded to excess and loathsome beyond expression in many instances. How fearful is war! I cannot put down the details he gave me, they are too horrible."

Mothers and wives, despite melancholy, rose to the occasion. In Montgomery, Alabama, southern matrons formed a Ladies Hospital Association in the early months of 1862. Sophia Gilmer Bibb, an industrious widow, organized women of the town to donate supplies, staff a hospital, and remain on call to take care of wounded soldiers and prisoners. Women in Columbia, South Carolina, transformed the state fairgrounds into a hospital, and the state college in town soon became a medical facility as well. One of the most famous Confederate nurses, Sally Tompkins, left her family plantation, Poplar Grove, to run a hospital in Richmond. Twenty-eight and unmarried when the war broke out, Tompkins was a devoted patriot. Her administration of the Robertson Hospital won her Confederate fans, including Jefferson Davis, who awarded her a military commission as "captain." Tompkins accepted her rank but refused a salary. Phoebe Pember, a socially prominent Jewish widow, superintended Chirimborazo Hospital in Richmond. Juliet Hopkins, wife of the

The retreat into Richmond from the battlefield at Seven Pines.

(BL)

chief justice of Alabama, performed such feats that she became known as the "Angel of the Confederacy." Wounded on the battlefield in May 1862, she spent the rest of her life with a limp from her wartime injury.

Many genteel women were exposed to scenes of ghastly horror when they went into hospital service. Kate Cumming of Mobile described a typical scene in April 1862: "The men are lying all over the house on their blankets, just as they were brought from the battle-field. They are in the hall, on the gallery, and crowded into very small rooms. The foul air from this mass of human beings at first made me giddy and sick, but I soon got over it. We have to walk, and when we give the men anything, kneel in blood and water." Ladies braced them-selves as they marched off to do their patriotic duties but still reeled from their exposure to such harsh, taxing conditions.

Wealthy men were expected to make even more dramatic sacrifices as they donned uniforms to counter the stereotype of a "rich man's war, poor man's fight." Several units demonstrated the patriotic loyalty of the planter class, such as the Magnolia Cadets in Selma, Alabama, manned entirely by local gentry. The privileged elite argued that class lines blurred during this time of crisis. As one Alabama woman described, "We were drawn together in a closer union, a ten-derer feeling of humanity linking us all together, both rich and poor."

While white men marched off to war, white families and slaves were expected to keep the plantation fires tended. Indeed, the planting of crops was considered a civilian priority, the back-bone of Confederate strategy. Women and slaves were enlisted in this effort to make the blockaded nation economically self-sufficient. Slave owners and small farmers alike were warned to "plant corn and be

free or plant cotton and be whipped."

With the onset of war, planters curbed their cotton production, cutting output in half between 1861 and 1862. Sugar planters, indigo planters, and other producers of cash crops were encouraged to curtail production in favor of raising foodstuffs. However, a small group of planters, who wanted to keep slaves prof-itable, were willing to trade with shady speculators and continued to warehouse and smuggle large cotton crops. Some, like Mississippian James Alcorn, saw the war as a boom time: "I can in five years make a larger fortune than ever; I know how to do it and will do it." Alcorn indeed made a killing in cotton.

Trying to keep slaves in order, trying to conduct agricultural and commercial activities during wartime disruption, absorbed the entire planter class. It is safe to say that on the home front, planters faced a long, slow defeat, like water on a rock, steadily wearing away.

The war turned power relations upside down on the home front. Kate McClure, a plantation mistress left behind in Union County, South Carolina, tired of the incompetence of her husband's overseer, Maybery, while McClure was away at

SOUTHERN CITIZENS OUTSIDE THEIR HOME ON CEDAR MOUNTAIN, VIRGINIA.

(LC)

war. She fired the hapless Maybery and deputized a slave, Jeff, to manage the work force. Indeed, the war offered many women the opportunity to exert more influence over plantation affairs, a challenge that many failed to embrace enthusiastically. They might gain some satisfaction from a job well done, but most mistresses were preoccupied with the dire straits of the southern wartime economy. Few escaped the melancholy dread of losing one or more family members to war.

Most southern plantation mistresses were trained to manage the planting oper-

ations. As the wives of wealthy men who served on the bench and in the legislature, they endured husbands' frequent and lengthy absences. The war, however, presented a different dilemma to mistresses left behind. Now they were faced with the possibility that their loved ones might not return—something rare in peacetime but all too common in war. Additionally, the threat of northern invasion undermined slave owners' authority, and most women found themselves not worried about prosperity but about survival as the war wore on. This crisis weighed heavily on planter wives, increasing their burdens as defeat seemed more and more inevitable.

The popular press advised ladies to elevate the sagging spirits of menfolk by throwing themselves into good works to help the Confederacy. Young girls buoyantly welcomed the challenge. Judith McGuire confessed: "Almost every girl plaits her own hat, and that of her father, brother, and lover, if she has the bad taste to have a lover out of the army, which no girl of spirit would do unless he is incapacitated by sickness or wounds." Such rhetoric exalted and enforced Confederate fervor, while stomping out dissent.

Wives and mothers, becoming more and more aware of the sacrifice such campaigns entailed, responded in time with misgivings to the call to arms. Alabama bride Mary Williamson cried over her husband's departure to the army: "This great sorrow makes me forget I ever had such a feeling as patriotism." Confederate ladies refrained from any public displays that might be interpreted as disloyalty. The

wife of the most revered soldier within the South, Mrs. Robert E. Lee, confided in a letter to her child: "The prospects before us are sad indeed as I think both parties are wrong in this fratricidal war." Whatever feelings she had in private, Mrs. Lee conveyed total support of her husband, as a friend commented: "I never saw her more cheerful, and she seems to have no doubt of our success." This split between the public and private aspects of women's feelings was prevalent among women of the planter class.

Confederates celebrated the ethic of self-sacrifice, like the matron who proclaimed, "We are ready to do away with all forms of work and wait on ourselves." But as hard times intensified, such sentiments withered. Many found it difficult to face the impossible dilemmas wartime presented. One woman confessed to her diary: "The real sorrows of war, like those of drunkenness, always fall most heavily upon women. They may not bear arms. They may not even share the triumphs which compensate their brethren for toil and suffering and danger. They must sit still and endure." Too few had the luxury of merely sitting still.

Desperate times produced desperate measures. Sallie Brock, the wife of a Confederate soldier, "was forced to go out into the woods nearby and with my two little boys pick up fagots to cook the scanty food left to me." Women reported giving up blankets and even cutting up carpets to send to the army for soldiers to sleep on. Patriot Katie Miller reported, "I told ma when *provisions* got so low that she couldn't feed a passing soldier to let me know every time one comes and I would go minus one meal for him."

Wartime papers were filled with ideas about women's sacrifice and heroism. One patriot in Mobile urged fellow Confederates to donate family jewels and silver. Another Alabama woman, the niece of James Madison, advised women to sell their hair to European wigmakers and donate profits to the government. A bounty of $2 million would be won if all would chop off two braids apiece at the going rate. She demanded: "*Let every patriot woman's head be shingled!*" Wartime hairstyles reveal that few heeded her call.

Southern plantations, which had been concerned with conspicuous consumption before the war, switched

dramatically into plants for production—
and in the case of luxury items, centers
for clever reproduction: persimmons for
dates, raspberry leaves for tea leaves, okra
seeds for coffee beans, cottonseed oil for
kerosene and beeswax for candlewax.
Many mistresses took to the woods, and
one memoirist recalled that the forest
became "our drug stores."

only supplies of the table. Wagons were
sent from Georgia with provisions which
the town distributed to those who came
for them. For hours there would be a
crowd of the best sort of people, standing
in line for their chance for a little bit of
something." In Atlanta, wartime deprivation was equally dire, as a matron
described: "I knew women to walk twen-

The search for necessities preoccupied most Confederate housewives, and
letters are filled with complaints and
advice concerning quinine, food, and
other valuables. Pooling resources was
important. Women in cities were especially hard-pressed, and most stood in long
lines for bread and even flour to make
bread. Charlestonian Louisa McCord
Smythe reported conditions in the blockaded port in 1863: "Food was frightfully
scarce and what there was of the coarsest
description. Bacon, cornbread made with
just salt and water, and biscuits made of
the wheat ground up whole, very coarse
and always with only salt and water to
mix them, were the staples, in fact the

ty miles for a half bushel of coarse, musty
meal with which to feed their starving little ones, and leave the impress of their
feet in blood on the stones of the wayside
ere they reached home again." One
woman who confronted the price of $70 a
barrel for flour exclaimed: "My God! How
can I pay such prices? I have seven children; what shall I do?" This cry echoed
throughout the Confederacy.

Speculators were targeted by angry
mobs. In April 1863, when a proprietor
refused to lower the price of bacon, a veteran's wife drew her pistol and allowed
fellow shoppers to "liberate" food supplies. After the fracas, witnesses—instead
of calling the police—established a fund

to provide food for indigent wives of soldiers. Donations were solicited through the local paper.

The looting of Confederate storerooms was a problem, especially in border states, where dissent and divides were open and flagrant. Also the Carolina and Tennessee backcountry was plagued by desertion and Confederate disloyalty that could and did end in bitter dispute. Where mountain folk were embittered by planter greed and disgusted by slave owners, mutiny ruled. In Marshall, North Carolina, rebel deserters broke into a government warehouse to obtain salt and even raided the house of a Confederate colonel. This set in motion a series of events which led to vicious reprisals and the Shelton Laurel Massacre when a dozen civilians accused of guerrilla warfare were captured and executed, including a thirteen-year-old boy and a sixty-year-old man. The Union campaign of starving out the rebels worked most effectively in this interior region.

While plantations were hard hit by the war in the rural South, we know relatively less about the way the war desiccated the lives of ordinary people. Commonly yeoman farms were stripped of sons, mules, tools, and other means of support, especially by the war's later years. Women took to the fields to keep their families fed because the southern countryside was ravaged.

Louisa Henry, anchored to her Mississippi River plantation, Arcadia, wrote to her mother in 1862: "I feel 10 years older than when the war commenced—and look at least five years older. I can see the change myself and my hair is turning gray rapidly." Two years later she had been driven off her planta-

tion and was hiding from federals in a cottage in the woods: "Ma, sometimes I feel *almost* desperate, and almost wish I could take a Rip Van Winkle sleep till all is over and settled."

Nineteen-year-old Amanda Worthington in Mississippi stopped writing in her diary for a year after her brother Bert died in the war but reflected when she recommenced: "What a change has passed over my life since last I kept a journal! Deep have I drank of the bitter waters of sorrow and the lightness of heart that once was mine will never return me more."

Confederate losses were enormous and devastating. The Union was winning

CONFEDERATE CHILDREN CAUGHT IN THE THROES OF WAR

Carrie Berry was too young to recall events in her home town of Atlanta when Georgia joined the Confederacy. But by 1864, when she turned ten, Berry reported the toll the war had taken. On her birthday, she revealed: "I did not have a cake. Times were too hard, so I celebrated with ironing. I hope by my next birthday we will have peace in our land so that I can have a nice dinner." Like those of many young white girls of the Confederacy, her formerly prosperous parents were unable to afford peace-time luxuries. In 1864 Margaret Junkin Preston of Virginia was shocked to report in a letter: "G. and H. at Sally White's birthday party: H. said they had 'white mush' on the table; on inquiry, I found out it was ice cream! Not having made any ice cream since wartimes, the child had never seen any, and so called it white mush."

Emma Le Conte reported in 1865 at the ripe old age of seventeen: "I have seen little of the lightheartedness and exuberant joy that people talk about as the natural heritage of youth. It is a hard school to be bred up in and I often wonder if I will ever have my share of fun and happiness." Some girls tried to look on the bright side. Amanda Worthington in rural Mississippi confided: "I think the war is teaching us some useful lessons—we are learning to dispense with many things and to manufacture other."

The war also taught children some terrible lessons. Cornelia Peake McDonald remembered her three-year-old wailing and clinging to her doll Fanny, crying that "the Yankees are coming to our house and they will capture me and Fanny." Another mother recounted a traumatic incident during Sherman's march. When Union soldiers invaded her home, her six-year-old daughter hid with her treasures—a bar of soap and her doll. "One of the men approached the bed, and finding it warm, in a dreadful language accused us of harboring and concealing a wounded rebel, and he swore he would have his heart's blood. He stooped to look under the bed, and seeing the little white figure crouching in a distant corner, caught her by one rosy little foot and dragged her forth. The child was too terror-stricken to cry, but clasped her little baby and her soap fast to her throbbing little heart. The man wrenched both from her and thrust the little one away with such violence that she fell against the bed."

Such scenes created vivid memories and tales oft repeated. So throughout the war, and the years to come, the mere mention of "Yankees" might strike terror in Confederate children, stimulating fears that haunted them in darkened bedrooms or around dying campfires.

the war through attrition—generals in gray almost always lost a greater percentage of their fighting force. By September 1862 the Confederate Congress was desperate enough to push through a draft law which raised the upper limit of conscription from the age of thirty-five to forty-five. The government compounded the problem by instituting the infamous "twenty Negro law" in October 1862, which exempted any white man from army service who could demonstrate a managerial role for twenty slaves or more—both owners and overseers quali-fied. (This happened shortly before the federal government similarly antagonized its people with a clause permitting substitutions for $300.) Poorer farm families were outraged that planters—who could afford service by buying substitutes—were now further legitimated if they sat out the war. These measures coincided with failing harvests and sparked sedition and unrest.

Within the Confederacy fewer than 5,000 men were granted government exemptions in nineteen categories ranging from occupational emergency (apothecaries) to physical disability (blindness, for example). And of those exempted, only 3 percent used the "twenty Negro law." On 85 percent of those plantations where white men could prove eligibility, no exemption was taken. Nevertheless, the perception of class privilege rankled the populace and created a public relations disaster. Even the $500 tax levied on exemptions, instituted in May 1863, failed to mollify critics.

By 1864, when plantation mistress Clara Bowen was joined by her husband for a week's furlough, she hoped he would not return to the front and wrote to a friend: "Do not call me unpatriotic, Alice! I am sure farmers are as necessary to our suffering country as soldiers. Food and clothing must be made for the army as well as for the women and children—starvation would be a more powrful foe than those we are now contending with." By the time Bowen wrote from Ashtabula, South Carolina, southern agriculture was already in ruins.

African American labor was being spirited away for the Union cause—men as soldiers and women as cooks and laundresses. African Americans also served as nurses in government hospitals, drivers of supply wagons and ambulances, and cooks and valets within Confederate camps—all slaves donated or supervised by masters. Most important, the War Department could and often did have the authority to impress slave labor into service. Louisa McCord Smythe recalled that her family slaves were requisitioned in wartime Carolina.

Slaves remained at the root of the problem during the prolonged battle for southern independence. Only in the last few weeks of the war was the Confederate government willing to consider arming blacks in a desperate bid to continue the losing battle. But by as early as 1863 the floodgates of freedom had opened wide to African Americans who seized the opportunity to escape masters.

Headquarters

53d Reg't N. C. Militia,

Fayetteville, April 18, 1862.

I am authorized by the Adjutant General of the State to purchase

DOUBLE-BARREL SHOT-GUNS and GOOD RIFLES,

for the use of the Militia of Cumberland county. Any persons having Guns of the proper description can get the full value in *Cash*, by passing them in to A. M. Johnson, Quartermaster, or Dr. Theo. Martine, Ordnance Officer of the Regiment. All Officers are requested to disseminate this information and to facilitate the purchase of Arms for the purpose named.

JOHN H. COOK,
Col. Com'dg.

WINCHESTER, VIRGINIA
—A TOWN THAT
CHANGED HANDS
FIFTY-TWO TIMES
DURING THE WAR.

(USAMHI)

This disintegrating process undermined the resolve of Confederates, especially non-slave owners who formed the majority of the fighting force. For those left behind on plantations, the process was even more painful to witness, as the spirit of emancipation created not so much a tidal wave of resistance as a strong and constant flow that washed over the South, eroding slaveholders' power with the sands of time, day by day.

The weakening of the Confederacy was most visible in those areas of the occupied South where escaped slaves, "contrabands," settled with families and expropriated Confederate lands, with the blessings of the federal government which leased property to blacks. On the South Carolina Sea Islands, a thriving community was established, what historian Willie Lee Rose has called a "rehearsal for Reconstruction." When federals conquered and secured the region in 1862, a community of ten thousand blacks were left behind. Many northern teachers moved in, including a young woman born into a prominent free black family in Philadelphia,

WITHOUT SLAVES, MANY
SOUTHERN FIELDS AND
PLANTATIONS WENT
UNTENDED.

(LC)

Charlotte Forten. Forten had been educated in Salem, Massachusetts, and become a teacher herself. She felt excited by the challenge of traveling south to help the freedpeople and settled in at St. Helena Island, the lone black among the colony of northern teachers. In May 1864 the *Atlantic Monthly* published a two-part article chronicling her experiment, "Life on the Sea Islands," which provides a vivid record of this dramatic episode. She found exceptional pupils: "I wish some of those persons at the North who say the race is hopelessly and naturally inferior could see the readiness with which these children, so long oppressed and deprived of every privilege, learn and understand." As this experiment proved successful, federal authorities sold some of the sea island property to blacks during auctions for unpaid taxes.

Another successful experiment was conducted at Davis Bend, Mississippi, on land owned by the family of the Confederate president. When Jefferson Davis's brother was forced to abandon his plantation in 1862, he was unable to convince his slaves to accompany him, and when Union troops arrived, blacks had both expropriated the Big House and managed to run the place efficiently. By 1865 these self-sufficient African Americans turned the place into what General Grant called "a negro paradise."

Many women expressed complex sentiments in the wake of this development, like the insightful Mary Chesnut, who commented on a slave insurrection: "I have never thought of being afraid of negroes. I had never injured any of them; why should they want to hurt me?" After her cousin was strangled by slaves on a nearby plantation, she further claimed: "But nobody is afraid of their own negroes. These [her cousin's murderers] are horrid brutes—savages, monsters—but I find everyone, like myself, ready to trust their own yard." Plantation women were trained to repress all fears of slaves, to maintain the pretense that enslaved African Americans were happy, childlike creatures.

Desertion of plantations by slaves was an integral part of wartime, and, ironically, as one woman complained, "those we loved best, and who loved us best—as we thought—were the first to leave."

Seventeen slaves fled the Wickham plantation in Hanover County, Virginia, in June 1862 and another seventeen were "carried off" between June 26 and July 5, 1863. Over 250 slaves remained behind, but Wickham believed this loss a considerable blow. Slaves fleeing behind enemy lines did not just represent a loss of income but equally a loss of face.

Why were African Americans so anxious to escape slavery if it was the pleasant paternalistic system owners painted it? Confederates again and again portrayed scenes of slave loyalty to defend themselves against Yankee charges. Eyewitness southern accounts provide occasional refutation of these tender scenes. Belle Edmondson described rounding up runaways in Shelby County, Tennessee: "A family of negroes had got this far on their journey from Hernando to Memphis when Mr. Brent met them, and they ordered him to surrender to a Negro, he fired five times, being all the loads he had—killed one Negro, wounded another, he ran in the woods and we saw nothing more of him—one of the women and a little boy succeeded in getting off also." For the first time since the American Revolution, large numbers of women and children found

freedom by deserting behind enemy lines. One mistress complained that slaves "in some cases have left the plantations in a perfect stampede."

A Union provost marshal reported in March 1864: "The wife of a colored recruit came into my Office tonight and says she has been severely beaten and driven from home by her master and owner. She has a child some two years old with her, and says she left two larger ones at home." Wives left to manage with depleting resources and a recalcitrant labor force took out their frustrations on remaining slaves. Emma Le Conte complained: "The

diers. We also have given hundreds of pairs of socks, the amount of 500, I think to the Army. Some three or four weeks since we sent twelve blankets, eight dozen pairs of socks, three carpet blankets, to Genl. Prices Army."

Besides the endless shipping of supplies, plantations were expected to host Confederate soldiers. Many gave generously to the anonymous sons of the Confederacy who imposed on their hospitality. Rebecca Ridley lived in the cookhouse of her former plantation Fair Mont, outside Murfeesborough, Tennessee, after Yankees burned her home. Following a battle she reported: "The ground has been covered with snow and ice—freezing our poor unprotected soldiers . . . poor fellows, how my heart bleeds for them. They come in at the houses to warm, and get something to eat, and some of our citizens who pretend to be very Southern grudge them the food they eat—say they will be eat out."

The burdens of contact with Yankees were unbearable to most southern white women. Cordelia Scales, on her plantation eight miles north of Holly Springs, Mississippi, reported a visit from the Kansas Jayhawkers: "They tore the ear rings out of ladies ears, pulled their rings

field negroes are in a dreadful state; they will not work, but either roam the country, or sit in their houses . . . I do not see how we are to live in this country without rule or regulation."

The lack of food and material comforts became so severe that some planters, to conserve supplies, simply turned slaves off the land. Mary Stribling reported that by the time of Lincoln's Emancipation Proclamation, her father had already warned slave women and children he would resort to selling those who could not earn their own keep. Much of the scarcity was a product of contributing to the Confederate cause, as one Mississippi mistress explained: "My heart has yearned over our brave, noble, bare-footed ragged young men, & have done all I could in my limited way to meet their necessities. Our stock of cloth laid up for the negroes is almost exhausted, having given suits of clothes to the sol-

& breast pins off, took them by the hair;
threw them down & knocked them about.
One of them sent me word that they shot
ladies as well as men & if I did not stop
talking to them so & displaying my
confederate flag, he'd blow my brains
out." Amanda Worthington, also on a
Mississippi plantation, told of the 20,000
bales of government cotton that went up
in flames with over a thousand head of
cattle and a thousand head of hogs and
ten thousand bushels of corn lost to pillaging Yankees.

Sarah Huff, in northern Georgia,
remembered that the "Yankees stripped us
bare of everything to eat; drove off all the
cattle, mules, horses; killed chickens; and
turned their horses into a wheat field so
that what the horses could not eat was
destroyed by trampling." Dolly Lunt
recalled a similar siege at her home near
Covington, Georgia: "But like demons
they rush in! My yards are full. To my
smoke house, my dairy, pantry, kitchen,
and cellar, like famished wolves they
come, breaking locks and whatever is in
their way." Mary Stribling in Fort Royal,
Virginia, was appalled at Yankee conduct:
"They came into the house and searched
it several times and stole various articles
of female apparel for which it is impossible to imagine what purpose they could
use them . . . they threatened the girls
with the worst treatment. They wrote all
over the walls addressing the ladies as if
they were writing a letter, they write low
pieces of obscenity to which they signed
Jeff Davis's name."

Some plantation houses in South
Carolina and other regions proudly display Yankee graffiti today to preserve the
defilement of their homes by soldiers who
clearly weren't "gentlemen." Graffiti was a

small problem compared to shelling.
Further, arson was an awful crime which
too many women witnessed. The savagery
of this torching policy prompted Henrietta
Lee to write directly to Union commander,
General David Hunter:

"Yesterday your underling, Captain
Martindale, of the First New York Cavalry,
executed your infamous order and burned
my house . . . the dwelling and every out-
building, seven in number, with their con-
tents being burned. I, therefore, a helpless
woman whom you have cruelly wronged,
address you, a Major General of the
United States Army, and demand why this
was done . . . . Hyena-like, you have torn
my heart to pieces! For all hallowed memories clustered around that homestead;
and demonlike, you have done it without
even the pretext of revenge . . . . Your
name will stand on history's pages as the
Hunter of weak women, and innocent
children: the Hunter to destroy defense-
less villages and beautiful homes—to
torture afresh the agonized hearts of
widows."

But not all contact with Yankees was
as brutal and hellish. Sallie Moore, a
Virginian, reported that when a Union
officer was inspecting a woman's home,
when climbing up the stairs "suddenly a
string broke and a shower of spoons and

forks came raining down the steps from under her hoops." In this tense moment, the soldier gallantly stooped to help the woman retrieve her silver, which he returned to her.

The testimony of southern blacks provides a powerful counterpoint to Confederate memoirs, as former slave Eliza Sparks of Virginia confided with special poignancy an encounter with a Yankee:

"I was nursin' my baby when I heard a gallopin', an' fo' I coud move here come de Yankees ridin' up . . . . The officer mought of been a general—he snap off his hat an bow low tome an' ast me ef dis was de way to Gloucester Ferry. Den he lean't over an' patted de baby on de haid an' ast what was its name. I told him it was Charlie, like his father. Den he ast, 'Charlie what' an' I told him Charlie sparks. Den he reach in his pocket an' pull out a copper an' say, 'Well, you sure have a purty baby. Buy him something with this; an' thankee fo' de direction. Goodbye, Mrs. Sparks.' Now what you think of dat? Dey all call me 'Mrs. Sparks!'

The slave presence was a troublesome issue for Confederate civilians. African Americans were both potential enemies as well as desperate allies within the plantation South. White women ironically might despair both over slaves running away and over slaves remaining behind to be looked after during federal invasion.

In the rich plantation region along the Combahee River in South Carolina, Union commander David Hunter, assisted by the intrepid scout and spy Harriet Tubman, recruited over 800 black soldiers during summer raids in 1863. By rousting slaves from their owners, spreading fear and mayhem in this and other successful operations, the North was able to wreak havoc with the plantation system—most effectively in the Mississippi Valley during the fall of 1863, when nearly 20,000 slaves deserted masters to join the Union army.

These forms of open rebellion were not as common as daily resistance. The enemies within came to represent as much of a threat to plantation productivity

BURIAL OF LATANÉ BY WILLIAM WASHINGTON (1864). WHEN THIS PAINTING WAS FIRST PUT ON DISPLAY, VIEWERS IN RICHMOND DROPPED COINS IN A BUCKET PLACED IN FRONT OF IT, TOUCHED BY THE THEME OF SACRIFICE.

(MC)

as invading foes. White southerners failed to grasp this reality until very late in the war. Indeed, by the time the tide had turned, some masters were forced to encourage slaves to run off—deprived of any means of feeding a dwindling work force. Especially in the battle-torn Virginia countryside, planters might record the number of runaways on a daily basis while northern troops crisscrossed the country.

Many black youth on plantations initially found the whole idea of war exotic and intriguing. Rachel Harris recalled, "I went with the white chillun and watched the soldiers marchin'. The drums was playing and the next thing I heerd, the war was gwine on. You could hear the guns just as plain. The soldiers went by just in droves from soon of a mornin' till sundown." But soon, the depletion of adult labor increased the burdens on slave children. Henry Nelson, only ten years old when the war broke out, remembered, "You know chillun them days, they made em do a man's work." Eliza Scantling, fifteen in 1865, remembered she "plowed a mule an' a wild un at dat. Sometimes me

hands get so cold I jes' cry."

For slave children the prospect of an invading enemy was confusing and, at times, terrifying. One slave remembered being told by the overseer when the slave was only ten years old that Yankees had "just one eye and dat right in de middle of the breast." Mittie Freeman, also ten, hid in a tree when the first bluecoats arrived. There is ample evidence to demonstrate that black children overcame apprehensions and even became enamored of Union soldiers in many instances. Although they might empathize with the adults' sense of jubilation over impending

IN TOWNS LARGE AND SMALL THROUGHOUT THE SOUTH, CITIZENS WOULD PROUDLY CHEER FOR THEIR BOYS MARCHING OFF TO WAR.

(HARPER'S WEEKLY)

AN ATLANTA MANSION, SCARRED BY SHELLING.

(LC)

freedom, at the same time they were children, overwhelmed and frightened by the prospect of any change. Additionally, carnage was close at hand, and many slave children witnessed frightening results. James Goings, only three when war broke out, recalled that by the end of the war "it wuzn't nuthin' to fin' a dead man in de woods."

Many black children sacrificed parents as well to the terrible conflict. As slave men fled the plantations, leaving wives and children behind, thousands were fatherless and hundreds were orphaned. Amie Lumpkin of South Carolina recalled her wartime loss: "My daddy go 'way to de war 'bout dis time, and my mammy and me stay in our cabin alone. She cry and wonder where he be, if he is well or he be killed, and one day we hear he is dead. My mammy, too, pass in a short time." Slave children made their unwilling offerings, too.

The southern cult of sacrifice began on a rather high note of camaraderie and fellowship within the Confederacy. Parthenia Hague described the way women in the Alabama countryside would gather for spinning bees: "sometimes as many as six or eight wheels would be whirring at the same time." Hague was heartened by these efforts, but another confided, "Slowly but surely the South was 'bled white.' Luxuries, there were none." The search for necessities preoccupied most southern housewives, and one girl in Winchester complained: "Out shopping all morning. I'd give a cent if Jennie Baker would quit sending for me to buy things for her. Its the bane of my existence for every store here in town is bare and nothing you want in there. Here today I walked all over town and couldn't get anything I wanted."

Pooling resources was a game that may have been a festive ritual early in the war, but by 1862 scarcity was worrisome, and by the summer of 1863 inflation and rationing made putting food on the table a major ordeal. Lucy Johnston Ambler fretted in summer 1863: "Indeed everything looks very gloomy. From having a comfortable table, I am reduced to bacon bone . . . I have a very sick grandchild and several servants sick with no suitable medicine." These stories were kept from menfolk away at war.

Women's sacrificial courage was summarized by Louisa McCord Smythe: "We would have died before we would complain to a man in the army. They had enough to bear without that." But after several seasons of war, no amount of sanitation could prevent soldiers from knowing the dire straits on the Confederate home front.

The constant cry for salt and bread echoed from the banks of the Shenandoah to the Delta and boomeranged back to the Confederate capital. A woman in Richmond wrote to a friend on April 4, 1863, in the wake of civil disturbances. She repeated the words of a young girl: "We are starving. As soon as enough of us get together we are going to the bakeries and each of us will take a loaf of bread. That is little enough for the government to give us after it has taken all our men." Nearly a thousand women and children banded together and "marched along silently and in order." They methodically emptied stores of goods and refused to stop even when the mayor confronted them to "read the Riot Act." The mob even ignored the city battalion. In desperation, Jefferson Davis appeared. The Confederate president was at first greeted with hisses, "but after he had spoken some little time with great kindness and sympathy, the women quietly moved on, taking their food with them." But over forty-eight hours later, an observer reported, "Women and children are still standing in the streets, demanding food, and the government is issuing to them rations of rice."

All of northern Virginia was alarmed by the Richmond Bread Riot and spread the word. One woman confided, "I am telling you of it because *not one word* has been said in the newspapers about it."

People throughout the countryside certainly understood the impulse. Virginia Cloud of Fort Royal complained, "I do not think the speculative spirit, so prevalent, is at all *patriotic*. I fear there are many who love *mammon* more than their country." There is evidence of widespread scapegoating during this period, and Jewish merchants in the Confederate capital were targeted by unhappy civilians. Government censorship suppressed news of such disturbances, but these incidents erupted spontaneously throughout the South.

Feeding the Confederacy and keeping the economy going was an increasingly impossible task. Women were reduced to dreams and wishes. Without food, without money, many women were perilously close to the abyss. Sarah Rice Pryor, a refugee outside Petersburg, gave birth during a blizzard over Christmas 1863. Mother and newborn were still bedridden three months later when her husband sought her out and found his wife and three children abandoned by the maid and being cared for by a hired hand. The furloughed soldier, in shock at the crumbling state of affairs, sold goods to raise cash to care for his wife. It was his desire that she never "again fall into the sad plight in which he had found me."

A NORTHERN ARTIST'S STARK IMAGE OF THE RICHMOND BREAD RIOT.

(FL)

From the war's opening hours on through to the end, Confederates employed dramatic religious rhetoric. A girl wrote to her cousin from South Carolina: "This is indeed a terrible war. How many hearts have been made desolate by its ravages. How many vacant places around the family altars. How terrible is the wrath of God, our sins as a people has brought this upon us and we should humble ourselves before Him. I

believe that Genl. Jackson was taken from us because we were making a god of him, not for any sin or unrighteousness in him, for I believe that he was not only doing good work as a soldier of our Confederacy but also of the cross." Jackson was indeed worshiped and revered during his military career. After death, he became a martyr and after the war canonized as part of the Confederate trinity: Davis, Lee, and Jackson.

Christian faith gave these women their redemption as well. They struggled mightily to find some sense of the slaughter, to the endless drumbeat of defeat. Eliza Andrews, after a visit to Andersonville Prison, worried about

vengeance: "I am afraid that God will suffer some terrible retribution to fall upon us for letting such things happen. If Yankees ever should come to South-West, Ga . . . and see the graves there, god have mercy on the land." This prophecy of doom perhaps came true in the form of William T. Sherman. Almost all white southerners recast Sherman's March as God's test of their faith. When Sherman's troops set off from Atlanta to Savannah, his men began in an orderly fashion, especially the first ten days, covering 275 miles. But after they reached Camp Lawton, a prisoner of war camp at Millen, many of the lawless brutalities emerged which made this campaign infamous.

Another severe test of faith came for many Confederates during the prolonged campaign to control Vicksburg, when thousands were caught up in the battle over this key port. This linchpin city on a bluff overlooking the Mississippi River had been the focus of federal military strategy for months. Union General Ulysses S. Grant finally gathered 70,000 to assault the CSA force of 28,000 in the summer of 1863. Before surrender, the besieged Confederates would be reduced to eating horses, dogs, and rats. The bombardment was so fierce that civilians dug caves into the mountainside for shelter. The memoir of Mary Ann Loughborough documented the genuine hardships of civilians. Loughborough recalled an incident when a shell lobbed into the center of a cave, crowded with families: "Our eyes were fastened upon it, while we expected every moment the terrific explosion would ensue. I pressed my child closer to my heart and drew nearer to the wall. Our fate seemed almost certain; and thus we remained for a moment with our

eyes fixed in terror on the missile of death, when George, the servant boy rushed forward, seized the shell, and threw it into the street, running swiftly in the opposite direction." Both George and the cave dwellers escaped injury.

Nerves frayed, supplies disappeared, and the determined Yanks maintained their attack. Scurvy, mule-skinning, and bombardment chipped away at morale. Wounded animals limped around looking for grass, evading butchers. Nightly shelling kept frightened children awake. The challenges were tremendous and daily life was precarious at best and, upon occasion, deadly.

Loughborough recalled a particularly awful day when one of the young girls, bored by confinement, ventured out: "On returning, an explosion sounded near her—one wild scream and she ran into her mother's presence, sinking like a wounded dove, the life

blood flowing over the light summer dress in crimson ripples from a death wound in her side caused by the shell fragment. A fragment had also struck and broke the arm of a little boy playing near the mouth of his mother's cave." She recalled the frequency of heartwrenching "moans of a mother for her dead child."

After countless dead, the Confederates hoisted the white flag on July 4, 1863. The soldiers were placated by the dignity they were accorded. As the half-dead men stacked their arms,

Life in Vicksburg

THE SHELL BY HOWARD PYLE, 1908

(MR. AND MRS. HOWARD P. BROKAW, PHOTOGRAPH COURTESY OF THE BRANDYWINE RIVER MUSEUM)

*M*ary Jane Sitterman was visiting her quartermaster husband in Vicksburg when she got trapped by the advancing Union army closing in on Vicksburg from the east. She became a cave dweller during the siege and left the following account:

"We . . . fitted the cave with the articles of housekeeping and were comfortably fixed. Our beds were arranged upon planks that were elevated on improvised stands, planks covered the ground floor, and these in turn were covered with matting and carpets. The walls surrounding the beds were also covered with strips of carpets, so all possible dampness was by a little care entirely eliminated. The wall carpeting was made adherent by small wooden pins or stobs."

Gordon Cotton, director of the Old Courthouse Museum in Vicksburg, relates the following in his *Vicksburg: Southern Stories of the Siege* (Vicksburg, 1988):

"Dora Miller noted that dogs and cats virtually disappeared from the streets and wondered where they went. In *The Daily Citizen*, Editor J. M. Swords described a dinner for eight shared by friends 'a delicious and featured rabbit' stew. He also pointedly mentioned that the cats had simultaneously disappeared and declared the felines of the city were an endangered species."

—Michael Ballard

witnesses detected a note of sympathy from their Union conquerors. The treaty, concluded on a federal holiday, contained generous terms and nearly all soldiers were paroled.

The defeat at Vicksburg and almost simultaneous Union victory at Gettysburg (with 15,000 casualties out of the 60,000 rebels engaged) seemed a dress rehearsal for the final surrender in April 1865. Many women by this fateful time sensed the doom on the horizon and began, consciously or unconsciously, to contemplate surrender. They continued to consolidate their own position as women worthy of Greek tragedy; indeed, one woman writer composed such a narrative with her novel: Augusta Jane Evans's *Macaria; or, Altars of Sacrifice* (1864). From this turning point in July 1863 to the treaty at Appomattox, hundreds of thousands were refugees, hundreds of thousands were wounded, and tens of thousands were buried. As they hoped and prayed for the final battle, few could contemplate life beyond war's end, afraid to anticipate the outcome.

Victories and Losses

Lee's surrender on April 9, 1865, ended the Confederate dream. The preservation of the Union gave Lincoln hope, a hope cut short by his assassination on April 14. The country, following Lincoln's wishes, rapidly tried to reunite, to heal the bitter wounds of four years of fratricide. Struggling back to peacetime was an enormous effort in the North but an even more devastating prospect for white southerners.

The war not only wiped out a generation (over one-fifth of the adult male white population in the South) but deprived descendants of misplaced dreams of returning to prewar prosperity. Ten billion dollars worth of property was destroyed in the region, but this "destruction" also reflected the emancipation of millions of slaves, many by their own liberation, and a new dawn for black hope. African Americans rejoiced in Confederate defeat. Slavery was abolished with the passage of the Thirteenth Amendment in December 1865, and citizenship rights were extended to individuals of the former slave class with the Fourteenth Amendment in July 1868. (Voting rights were reinforced by the Fifteenth Amendment, ratified in 1870.) These legislative strides on the federal level did little to better race relations during the social and political ferment that followed war's end. Indeed, many southern politicians defied the spirit of these constitutional amendments and enacted "Black Codes," as they came to be known—laws meant to prevent African American freedom.

The Freedmen's Bureau, established during wartime under the leadership of General O. O. Howard (after whom Howard University is named), and various war relief agencies tried to move into the shambles of the postwar South to set up schools, to protect voting rights, and to initiate economic self-sufficiency among African Americans. During the summer of 1865 the Freedmen's Bureau distributed 150,000 daily rations (nearly 50,000 to whites), a necessity that seemed to grow

rather than diminish as the agency passed out nearly twenty-two million rations between 1865 and 1870.

Defeated Confederates reeled from the consequences of their failed rebellion. Once rich Delta lands were filled with weeds and burned out shells of former estates. This was in direct contrast to the stellar record of agricultural production enjoyed in the North, where wheat production beat prewar output, and corn, pork, and beef exports doubled, while the Union supplied its armies and its people.

Transportation and industrialization boomed. Only the textile industry suffered in the North (because of the shortage of raw material). Coal production, copper processing, and other resources accelerated from wartime demand. So much commercial growth contributed to the Civil War being called "the Second American Revolution." Although economic output may have slowed in some areas, the overall picture in the 1860s is one of acute acceleration. Economists debate the question of growth during the war years, but all agree that the sectional redistribution of wealth was enormous. In 1860 the per capita wealth of white southerners was 95 percent higher than that of northern

45

whites. That situation was reversed dramatically in 1870 when the northern per capita wealth was 44 percent greater than that of southern whites. The South's share of the national wealth had been 30 percent in 1860 but shrank to 12 percent in 1870.

The back of the plantation economy had been broken, and there seemed no way to restore prewar patterns, despite planters' dreams. The black work force was reluctant to return to former plantations. Although most wanted to escape fieldwork, without education and resources, the majority were forced into daily wage labor. Indeed, the sharecropping system was seen as a means to property owning by land-hungry freedpeople. By war's end, blacks discovered that "forty acres and a mule" was a dream rather than any federal agenda. President Andrew Johnson's amnesty programs and congressional caution prevented the federal government from allowing distribution of public lands, which were plentiful. The land for black ownership need not have come from any property held by whites. But the principle of white supremacy reigned. Northern intervention may have allowed occasional interlopers such as the first generation of black elected officials during Reconstruction, including Hiram Revels and Francis L. Cardozo. The specter of black judges, black legislators, and African Americans as local federal officeholders alarmed former Confederates.

White men felt undermined and

overwhelmed in the wake of surrender. The 1870 census revealed 36,000 more women than men in Georgia and 25,000 more in North Carolina. In Atlanta more than 8,000 families, many headed by women, were utterly destitute in the wake of the war. Federal troops were a constant and visible reminder of Confederate defeat. Georgian Fanny Andrews commented on women pulling their drapes, feigning mourning. White women boy-

cotted social functions where soldiers might appear, including church, where they felt sermons were influenced by the federal presence.

During the summer and fall of 1865 many Confederates fled their former homes. Brazil and Mexico hosted colonies of disenchanted former slave owners, and Europe welcomed these aristocrats in exile as well. Hundreds also crossed the Canadian border as refugees. But the majority of white southerners remained in their defeated homeland.

One Georgia woman reported, "The pinch of want is making itself felt more severely every day and we haven't the thought that we are suffering for our country that buoyed us up during the war." Widows in the South were deprived of the generous pensions provided families of Yankee veterans. Despite poverty, white southerners stubbornly held on to their pride. Many refused to take the dreaded oath (renouncing the Confederacy and pledging loyalty to the Union) and sought federal pardons from Lincoln's successor, Andrew Johnson, who proved an all too lenient dispenser of mercy. Surprisingly, only Confederate president Jefferson Davis served any time in jail and only one Confederate officer, the infamous Commander Henry Wirz, in charge of the Andersonville Prison, was executed for war crimes. So despite Confederate complaints to the contrary, the federal government proved amazingly tolerant following Union victory.

As Lincoln had predicted, once the Union was preserved, the difficulty would be to restore the nation to order. Most ex-Confederates wished to embalm their status by exalting the nobility of the Lost Cause. Women were especially active in these campaigns to rewrite history, praise southern military heroes, and paint a picture of glory and honor in the wake of such a serious setback as presidential and congressional Reconstruction. The United Daughters of the Confederacy and other memorial organizations kept the Confederate cause alive well into the next century. Indeed, it wasn't until the corrupt bargain in the wake of the election of 1876 that the South wholly rejoined national politics, and at the cost of black political progress, as many critics have pointed out.

But despite these setbacks, Reconstruction gave African Americans as a group their first taste of freedom, and many seized the moment with vigor and admirable restraint. The way southern blacks struggled for their rights and stepped lively into political arenas is one of the great political transformations of the millennium. Whatever happened in the backlash that followed, former slaves shed their shackles, bidding for their full and rightful place in the public sphere.

Following the war, many former Confederate states were forced to contend with the discomforts of modernization. Folkways could be supplanted by federal directives. State governments grappled with education and reform in ways that had never been seen before south of the

Mason-Dixon line. The forced march toward fuller political participation, literacy, and agricultural and labor reforms pulled an unruly region more into line with its northern neighbor.

The wartime Congress could be proud of many accomplishments. Certainly, the Homestead Act had far-reaching effects as over 500,000 settled 80 million acres by the end of the century. Additionally, the Morrill Act paved the way for the state university system. After 1862 states were granted public lands (amounts based on a per legislator basis) for sale, and money raised established land-grant colleges. This was the most important and initial grant of federal aid to education. Land grants to the railroads totaled over 120 million acres. The steady march of progress created a parade of modern legislative victories ushering in national banking, homesteading, colleges and universities, railroads, and, finally, the Internal Revenue Act.

Nevertheless, the costs of war were enormous. The Civil War resulted in more soldiers dying than were killed in almost all subsequent wars in American history. Almost 630,000 died, with over half a million wounded. At Antietam on a single day nearly 4,800 were killed, whereas less than 4,000 Americans died during the Revolutionary War. But the impact on the national scale paled in comparison to the effect on local com-

munities: in Worcester, Massachusetts, over 4,000 of its eligible male population of 24,000 went to war and nearly 500 never came back. Most homecoming reunions among Yankee soldiers were touching rather than melodramatic affairs, as Leander Stillwell recalled. When he returned to Otterville, Indiana, Stillwell was happily restored to his parental home: "We all had a feeling of profound contentment and satisfaction . . . too deep to be expressed by mere words." The next day he took off his uniform

CLARA BARTON'S POSTWAR CRUSADE TRACING MISSING SOLDIERS

Once the war was over in April 1865, many families faced the harsh reality that their husbands and brothers, fathers and sons might not be coming home. Tens of thousands had not heard from families for months or even years and found their inquiries to the government failed to elicit response because the War Department was flooded with requests following Confederate surrender. Certainly the work of identifying the thousands buried in anonymous graves would never be completed, but Union women dedicated themselves to trying.

Clara Barton, whose legendary war work had saved hundreds of soldiers' lives, established a clearinghouse for the purpose of tracing lost soldiers. This task propelled her into a controversial tangle of issues. She began her operation even before government funds were set aside for the task. Her search for the missing naturally led to Andersonville, the notorious Confederate prison where so many Union soldiers has lost their lives. She traveled to Georgia in the summer of 1865 to help identify remains and rebury the dead. But Barton found her plans thwarted by military resistance. Caught in a bureaucratic crossfire, she was not appointed head of a Bureau of Missing Persons but found herself at odds with the War Department.

Having fought military red tape throughout the war, Barton simply sidestepped the chain of command and launched a private crusade — advertising in newspapers, printing circulars with lists of missing men, reaching out directly to those anxious families seeking assistance.

Barton's crusade stirred up enormous passion. She was able to locate information on dying men soliciting soldiers who may have witnessed a comrade's passing, so that details of death were conveyed to anxious mothers who begged to know how their sons had died. She also was able to sift through enemy records and discover burial information on thousands, especially those who perished in prisons, letting wives know that their husbands would not be coming home but also letting the government know a veteran had died.

On occasion, Barton would track down a soldier who had disappeared for his own reasons. In one case, a veteran raged at Barton for having his name "Blazoned all over the Country" and said his family could just wait until he was ready to contact them. Barton sent a stinging reply, notifying him, "Your mother died waiting." Much more often, Barton was an instrument of welcome reunion.

Congress finally recognized the significance of Barton's campaign and appropriated $15,000. But by the time she closed down her operation in 1869, Barton had spent all the government money and nearly $2,000 of her own funds. She went without salary as she and her staff processed over 63,000 letters, providing more than 22,000 families with information on missing soldiers. Through her efforts many families were able to bury their dead and move on with their lives.

CLARA BARTON

(NA)

(shedding his status as a Union lieutenant), put on his father's old clothes, and "proceeded to wage war on the standing corn."

But not all soldiers had a homecoming. Over twelve thousand of the Iowa men who enlisted (half of all eligible) died: 3,500 on the battlefield, 500 in prison, 8,500 from disease. Over 8,500 of those who went home returned seriously disabled. In the four years of war, almost 30,000 amputations were performed. In the state of Mississippi, 20 percent of the state revenue was spent on artificial limbs in 1866. Private Cutler Rist of the Thirty-Sixth Wisconsin had his tibia shattered by a bullet at Cold Harbor on June 1, 1864. Two days later surgeons removed his leg from the knee down. He was operated on again in December 1864, when leaking fluid indicated the possibility of gangrene. Discharged in May 1865, he hobbled home to Madison, Wisconsin. Rist, like thousands of other soldiers, would have a permanent reminder of his war service.

Nervous diseases rapidly multiplied

in the postwar years, causing physician S. Weir Mitchell to complain about "epileptics . . . every kind of nerve wound, palsies, choreas, stump disorders. I sometimes wonder how we stood it." Causes and treatment of mental illnesses were little understood during the late to mid-nineteenth century. A surprisingly small number, a little over 800 men, were discharged from the Union army because of mental disabilities. Despite this low number, one medical authority at the time complained that "the number of cases of insanity in our army is astonishing." Less than 2,500 cases of mental illness were reported in the North during the entire war, and some doctors suggested that they thought the war actually reduced mental diseases. The director of a District of Columbia asylum offered conjecture: "The

mind of the country was raised by the war to a healthier tension and more earnest devotion to healthier objects than was largely the case amid the apathies and self-indulgences of the long-continued peace and prosperity that preceded the great struggle." The war, an Ohio doctor suggested, channeled energies into "new and important spheres."

We do have evidence that opium addiction increased: not only veterans but their wives became dependent on the drug. Horace Day argued in his 1868 medical text that opiates offered temporary relief to those "maimed and shattered survivors from a hundred battlefields,

diseased and disabled soldiers released from hostile prisons, anguished and hopeless wives and mothers, made so by the slaughter of those who were dearest to them."

The war took an enormous emotional toll, as children lost their childhoods, families lost loved ones, and the nation mourned the passing of a generation of youth who could have given talents and energies and not just their bodies to their beloved country. Like many other wars, the scars were deep and not all visible. Burying the dead did not always bury the memories, and the words of soldiers and loved ones continue to haunt. The impact of this terrible contest remains very much with us today, as statues of Civil War soldiers dot town squares from rural New England to bustling Manhattan. As Americans moving into the twenty-first century, our reflections on the terrible ordeal that almost tore the country apart seem nostalgic. Yet our constant reexamination of those issues for which so many died and so many more fought, to appreciate the bravery of those on the home front as well as the battlefront, signals the strengths of our American heritage, as we are condemned not to relive our history but to fulfill the promise of our victories and recall the memories of losses.